# The Simple Facts of
# SIMPLE MACHINES

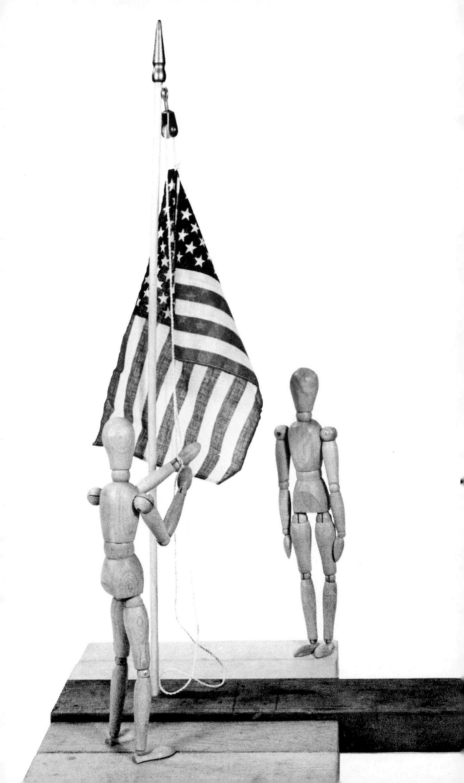

# The Simple Facts of SIMPLE MACHINES

## Elizabeth James & Carol Barkin

Photographs by DANIEL DORN, JR.

Diagrams by SUSAN STAN

LOTHROP, LEE & SHEPARD CO. / New York

# To David and Coleman

Printed in the United States of America.

2  3  4  5

**Library of Congress Cataloging in Publication Data**

James, Elizabeth

The simple facts of simple machines.

SUMMARY: Describes the simple machines—lever, pulley, wedge, screw, inclined plane, and wheel and axle—and explains how they make work easier.
1. Machinery—Juvenile literature. [1. Machinery]
I. Barkin, Carol, joint author.  II. Title.
TJ147.M28      531'.8      74-20664
ISBN 0-688-41685-3
ISBN 0-688-51685-8 (lib. bdg.)

# Contents

# 1
# Machines and Work

When you think about machines, you probably think of cars, airplanes, and cement mixers. Maybe you think of vacuum cleaners, washing machines, and power saws.

All these machines need motors to make them run. But there are machines that don't need motors —machines like hammers and nails, egg beaters, scissors, and bottle openers.

These things need only a person to make them run. They don't need any other kind of power. Are they really machines?

Yes, because like all machines, they help people do some kind of work. They are **simple machines**.

There are six kinds of simple machines. All of these help people do work.

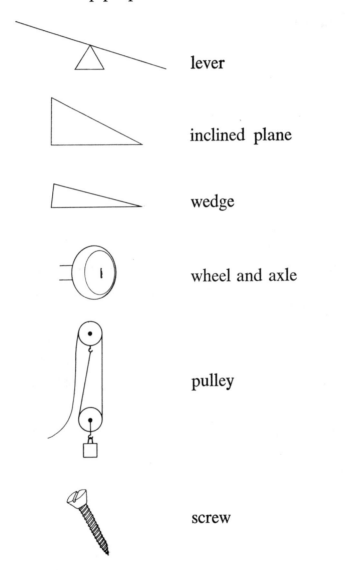

lever

inclined plane

wedge

wheel and axle

pulley

screw

Everyone knows what work is. Men and women may go to work in the morning. Students may do homework. Everybody helps with housework.

All of these are different kinds of work.

But when we talk about machines, we use the word "work" in a special way. This kind of work has two parts.

One part is how much **force** is needed to do the work.

The other is how far the force is used. This is the **distance**.

If you lift a book from the floor to the table, you are doing work. You have to use **force** to lift the book, and you must use this force for the **distance** between the floor and the table.

If you lift the same book from the floor to a high shelf, you are doing more work. You are using the same **force** for a longer **distance**.

Now try lifting five books from the floor to the table. This is more work than lifting one book from the floor to the table, because it takes more **force** to lift five books the same **distance**.

What if you lift all five books to the high shelf? This is even more work.

If you think about force and distance, many of the things you do every day can be called work.

Most of them aren't very hard work, though. It's easy for you to lift the books to the table or even to the shelf. You don't need a machine to help you. But there are many things you can't do by yourself.

You can't lift up a car by yourself to fix a flat tire. But you can do it if you use a jack. A jack is a machine. Using this machine gives you more **force**.

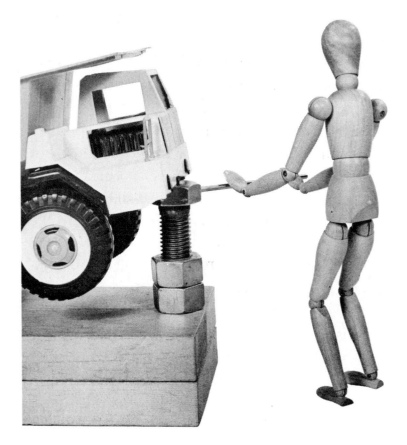

A bicycle is another kind of machine. You can probably run fast. But you can go much faster on a bike. Using this machine, you can go a longer **distance** in the same amount of time, which means that it gives you more speed.

Simple machines can help you do work in two important ways. They can:

give you more force, or

give you more distance or speed.

Many simple machines can also be used to change the direction of force. This does not help you do more work, because it doesn't change the force or the distance. But it is often more convenient, for instance, to pull down in order to lift something up.

# **2**
# Levers

A **lever** is a simple machine. It is a stiff bar that turns on a point. The point is called the fulcrum. The bar moves but the fulcrum does not. The lever can help you do work. It uses force and distance.

You can use your force to lift five books from the floor to the table. That's easy. But you probably can't lift your mother, even if you use all your force. Lifting your mother is too much work for you to do by yourself. But you could lift her with a lever.

A seesaw can be a lever. The board is the bar. The stand that holds it up is the fulcrum.

12

If your mother sits in the middle of her side of the seesaw and you push down on the middle of your side, you can't lift her.

But if she stays in the middle of her side and you push down on the *end* of your side, you can lift her off the ground.

You can see that on the seesaw you move farther than your mother does. The distance you go is more than the distance you make her go. And the farther your force is from the fulcrum, the more distance you must use. As the distance you use increases, the amount of force you need decreases.

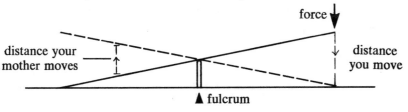

Using the lever, you can do more work with your force. But you must use more distance. You are trading distance for force.

13

Try making a lever to lift things. All you need is a board and something to rest it on. By moving your force closer to or farther from the fulcrum, see how much work you can do. If you don't have a board handy, you can make a small lever by resting a ruler on the handle of a spoon.

What are some other levers?

A crowbar is a lever that helps lift heavy things. If your wagon were heavily loaded and one of its wheels got stuck in the mud, you could use a crowbar to get it out. The crowbar rests on a hump of ground or a rock, which is its fulcrum. To make the crowbar work, the fulcrum must be very close to the wagon wheel. You push your end of the crowbar down through more distance than the other end moves, but you don't need to use much force.

A claw hammer is a lever that helps pull out nails. The fulcrum at the top of the hammer doesn't move. The handle and the claw of the hammer make the lever. This is a curved lever, but it works the same way as a straight one.

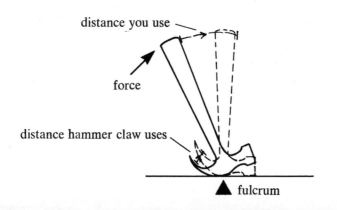

You use force to push on the end of the handle, and the claws pull out the nail.

It is easier to pull out a nail with a long-handled hammer than with a short one. The longer handle uses more distance and so you need less force.

A seesaw, a crowbar, and a claw hammer are all the same kind of lever. In all of them the fulcrum is between the force and the thing you want to move.

You've probably noticed that this kind of lever, which has the fulcrum between the force and the thing you want to move, changes the direction of force. You push down on one side of the lever in order to make the other side go up. But this change by itself does not help you do more work.

There are two other kinds of levers.

One kind has the fulcrum at one end and the

15

force at the other end. In this kind of lever the thing you want to move is between the force and the fulcrum.

You can make this kind of lever with a board. Put your end of the board on a box or a rock. Then ask a friend to sit on the board.

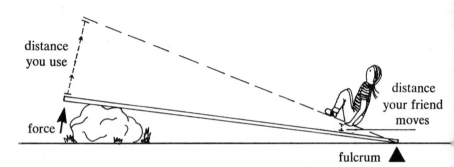

When you use force to lift your end of the board, you lift your friend off the ground.

The other end of the board is the fulcrum. It stays on the ground and doesn't move.

Lifting your friend is work. If he sits too close to your end of the board you may not have enough force to lift him. If he sits close to the fulcrum the machine helps you do the work with less force.

But you must use your force for a longer distance. Your end of the board will have to move farther than your friend moves. You are trading distance for force when you use this lever.

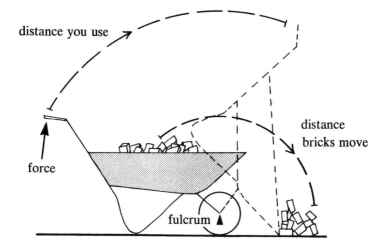

A wheelbarrow is this kind of lever. When you dump a load of heavy bricks out of a wheelbarrow, you move the wheelbarrow's handles through more distance than the bricks move. But you don't need as much force as you would if you tried to move the whole load of bricks without a lever.

A bottle opener also is this kind of lever. In a bottle opener, the fulcrum is the end that touches the top of the bottle cap. You use force at the other

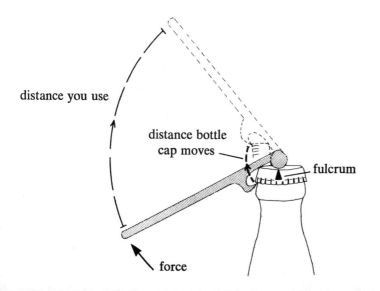

end. The bottle cap is pulled up by the hook near the fulcrum. The hook is between the fulcrum and the force.

Unlike the first kind of lever, levers in which the thing you want to move is between the fulcrum and the force do not change the direction of your force. You pull up at the end and the part of the lever that lifts things also goes up.

The third kind of lever has the fulcrum at one end and the thing you want to move at the other end. The force is between them.

A fishing pole is this kind of lever. The fulcrum is the handle end of the pole that rests against your body. The thing you want to move is the fish that is attached to the other end of the pole. You use force between the handle and the fish.

When you use this kind of lever, you aren't trying to move something that is too heavy. Instead, you are trying to move something farther, through more distance. The end of the pole moves farther than the part where you use your force.

You are trading force for distance when you use this lever. But you are still doing work.

When you play baseball or tennis, you also use this kind of lever. Your shoulder is the fulcrum and your arm provides the force. The end of the bat or racquet swings through more distance than your arm does in the same amount of time. This means that the end of your bat is moving faster than your arm. So this kind of lever gives you more speed. But again, it does not change the direction of your force.

Sometimes two levers are used together. A pair of scissors is two levers attached to each other. The place where they are attached is the fulcrum. The fulcrum is between the cutting blades and the force.

19

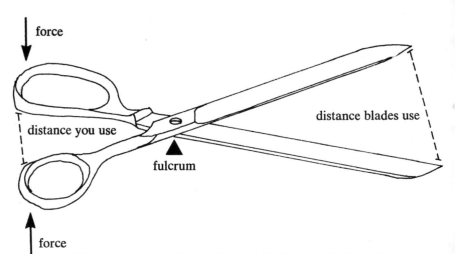

Some scissors have long blades and short handles. They are used to cut thin materials like paper or cloth, which doesn't take much force. The blades move through more distance than the handles. You are trading force for distance.

But sometimes scissors help you trade distance for force. If you try to cut a piece of heavy cardboard, it is easier to cut if you put the cardboard close to the fulcrum of the scissors. Then the handles where you use force move farther, through more distance, than the cutting blades.

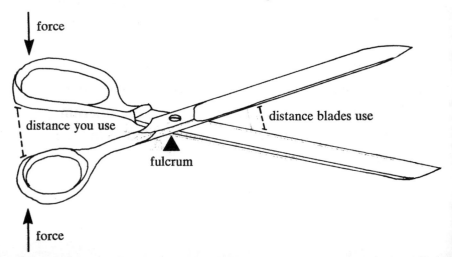

Tin snips have very long handles and very short blades. They cut metal that you can't break by yourself. The handles move much farther than the blades.

A pair of pliers is also two levers. The handles move through more distance to give more force at the short ends.

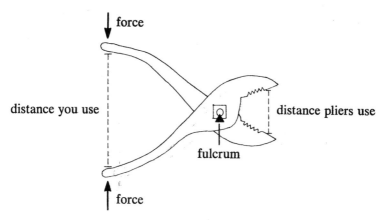

A nutcracker is made of two levers. The two jaws of the nutcracker are attached at the fulcrum. When you use force at the handles, you can crack a hard nut. The closer the nut is to the fulcrum, the easier it is to crack.

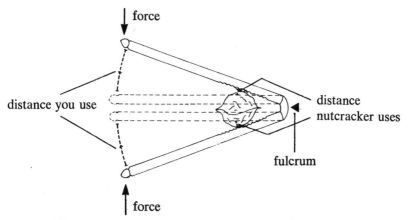

The ends where you use your force move farther than the parts that crack the nut. Again, you are trading distance for force when you use this lever.

The three kinds of levers are simple machines that can help you do work. You can make a lever to trade distance for force or force for distance.

# 3
# Inclined
# Planes

The inclined plane is another simple machine. "Inclined" means "at an angle" and "plane" means "flat surface." So an inclined plane is a slope or ramp.

This machine does not move. But it helps you move or raise things that are too heavy. Using an inclined plane, you can do more work with your own force, but you must use more distance.

Suppose you want to lift a big box of books into the back of a station wagon. But the box is too heavy to lift straight up. You can use an inclined

plane to do this work. Put one end of a board on the tailgate and the other end on the ground. Then your force is enough to push the box up this inclined plane. You can see that the distance the box travels along the board is more than the distance from the ground to the tailgate. You are trading distance for force.

distance you use

force

distance from ground to tailgate

If you use a longer board to make the inclined plane, you need even less force to move the box into the station wagon. But you have to move the box over a longer distance.

24

The inclined plane on the right has a steeper angle of slope.

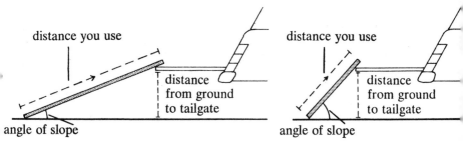

distance you use

distance from ground to tailgate

angle of slope

distance you use

distance from ground to tailgate

angle of slope

The longer the board, the flatter the angle of the inclined plane. This is called the angle of slope. A shorter board has a steeper angle. A steeper or larger angle of slope requires more force but less distance. And, of course, as the angle of slope gets flatter or smaller, the distance increases but less force is needed.

An inclined plane cannot change the direction of your force. You push up at an angle in order to move something in the same direction.

You see inclined planes every day, even though you may not think of them as machines. A driveway is a machine that helps people get cars, baby

carriages, or bicycles up to the sidewalk level from the street. It's easier to push your bike up a driveway than to lift it up the step of the curb, but the driveway is longer. You must use more distance.

Many ball parks have both ramps and stairways from one deck up to the next. The ramp is longer than the stairway and it has a shallower angle of slope. So it's easier to walk up the ramp but it will probably take longer since you have to walk farther.

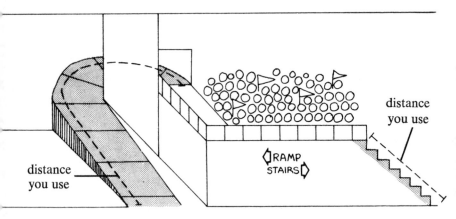

The ramp has a shallower angle of slope than the stairway.

But a flight of stairs itself is an inclined plane. It is less work to climb a flight of stairs from the first floor to the second floor than it is to climb

straight up a ladder. In stairways, too, the smaller
the angle of slope, the less force is needed, but the
distance you travel is greater. Older people often
find it easier to move their bodies up a long flight
of shallow steps than a short flight of steep steps.
And you may be grateful for a long, shallow in-
cline as you bicycle up a mountain road.

The ladder has a steeper angle than either of the stairways.

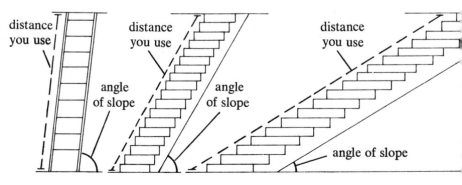

distance
you use

angle
of slope

distance
you use

angle
of slope

distance
you use

angle of slope

# 4
# Wedges

A wedge is made up of two inclined planes. But this machine is used in a different way. Unlike the inclined plane, which does not move, the wedge is moved by force through distance.

Wedges can be used to help you lift things. You can see how a wedge helps to lift something if you try to lift a very heavy box off the ground. You can't get your fingers under the box to get a grip on it. But you can push a wedge under the box to raise it enough to grip it.

You can see that the distance you must push the wedge is more than the distance that the box

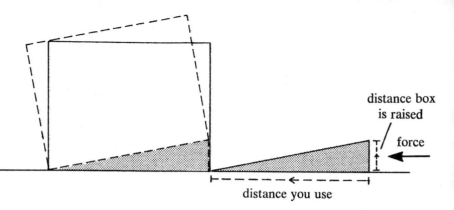

distance box is raised

force

distance you use

is raised. But you need less force to push the wedge in than you would need to lift the box straight up.

Like the inclined plane, the longer the wedge and the smaller the angle of slope, the less force is needed, but the wedge must be pushed through

The shorter wedge has a larger angle of slope, but both wedges raise the box the same distance.

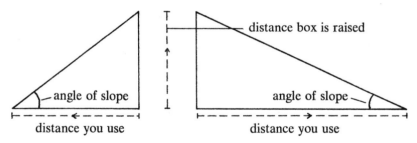

angle of slope

distance you use

distance box is raised

angle of slope

distance you use

a greater distance. You can use a longer wedge to raise the box the same amount. You will need less force to do the same work, but you will push the wedge through more distance.

A wedge changes the direction of your force. When you push forward, the inclined planes of the wedge push up and down.

29

Sometimes you can use your fingers or your foot as a wedge, but they are not thin enough to push under very heavy things. Also, a wedge must be stiff enough to hold the weight without bending or breaking.

Wedges can also be used to tighten or hold things in place. Farmers often tap wooden wedges into the holes in fence posts to tighten loose rails. If you have a loose chair rung, you can tighten it by pushing a small wedge into the hole where the rung fits in.

Wedges are most often used to push things apart. A nail is a wedge that pushes wood apart as you pound it in. Remember that wedges change the direction of your force: as you pound a nail down, the wood is pushed apart sideways.

When you pound a nail into a board, you only want to push the wood far enough apart to get the whole nail in. Only the pointed end of the nail is the wedge.

force

distance you use

distance wood is pushed apart

Remember that the smaller the angle of slope, the less force you need to push the wedge in, but you must push it through more distance. This means that if you have two nails of the same thickness, the one with the longer point is easier to pound in than the one with the shorter point; the longer wedge has a smaller angle of slope. Both

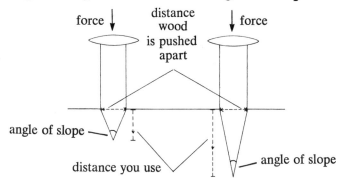

nails push the wood apart the same amount—they do the same work. The nail with the longer point moves through more distance, and this means you need to use less force.

Chisels too are used to push wood apart. A very sharp chisel has a smaller angle of slope than a chisel that has a blunter edge. So you need less

You must use more distance with the sharper chisel.

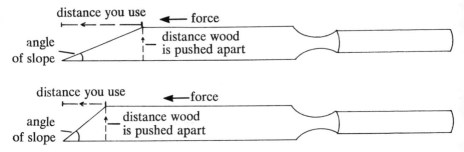

force to use the sharp chisel, but you have to push it through more distance to make a cut of the same depth.

In fact, the blades of all cutting tools like knives, saws, and axes are really wedges that push things apart. When you sharpen the blade of a cutting tool, you make the wedge thinner and longer, and the angle of slope gets smaller. This means less force is needed to use the wedge.

Many tools are combinations of two simple machines, the wedge and the lever. You have already seen that a pair of scissors is two levers joined at the fulcrum. The blade edges of the scissors are wedges. An ax, too, combines a wedge and a lever. It is the same kind of lever as a baseball bat.

When you sharpen the blade of a knife, the angle of slope gets smaller and the wedge gets longer.

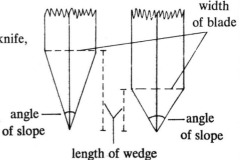

A can opener that punches holes in a can's top combines a wedge and a lever. The pointed end is a wedge that cuts the metal apart. The fulcrum is the hook that fits under the rim of the can. As you pull up on your end of this lever, the wedge end goes down through the top of the can.

This might seem like the same kind of lever as the bottle opener, but if you look carefully at how they work you can see that they are really two different kinds of levers. In the bottle opener, the fulcrum is at one end of the lever and the direction of your force is not changed—the edge of the bottle cap comes up as you pull the end of the lever up. But in the punch-top can opener, the fulcrum is between the two ends of the lever, and as you remember, this kind of lever changes the direction of your force.

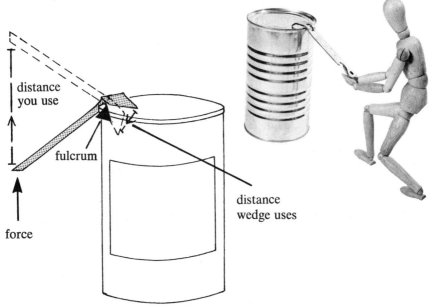

distance you use

fulcrum

force

distance wedge uses

# 5
# Wheel
# and
# Axles

You use wheels every day in things like roller skates, wagons, scooters, and furniture casters. This kind of wheel does not do the same work as the simple machine called the wheel and axle. Its purpose is to reduce friction.

Friction is created when two things rub against each other. A wheel, which rolls instead of dragging on the ground, lessens friction. When you put on your bicycle's brakes, the wheels lock. This increases friction between the tire and the ground and slows the bicycle.

The wheel and axle is a simple machine made

up of a small wheel attached to the center of a larger wheel. The small wheel is the axle; it is usually a rod that turns as the larger wheel turns.

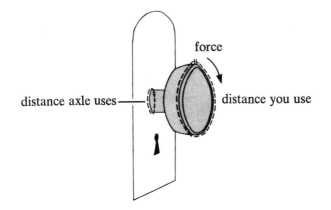

A wheel and axle can be used to increase force. A doorknob is a wheel and axle in which the knob is the wheel and the rod through the door is the axle. When you turn the knob, the rod also turns and moves the catch of the door. If you remove the knob, you will find that the rod is very hard to turn with your fingers. The knob is much bigger around than the rod and you must move it through more distance, but it needs less force.

A well bucket is raised by a wheel and axle called a windlass. It is easier to turn the large wheel than to turn the axle across the well, but you must turn the wheel through more distance. You are trading distance for force.

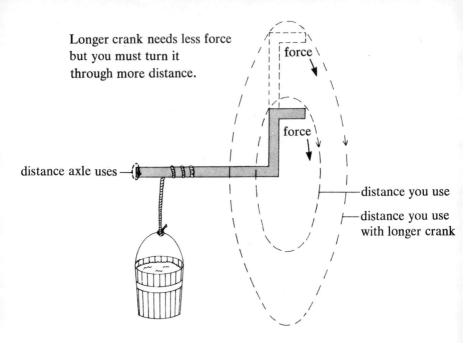

Longer crank needs less force but you must turn it through more distance.

force

force

distance axle uses

distance you use

distance you use with longer crank

A windlass often has a handle to turn the wheel. You could make a windlass with only a crank attached to the axle. But as you turn it in a circular motion, you are still using a wheel and axle. The

wheel is imaginary. A longer crank moving through a larger circle needs even less force but more distance.

Wrenches and skate keys are also wheels and axles, but in this case the axle is the thing you want to turn. That is why skate keys are cut to fit exactly around the nut of the skate, and wrenches can be tightened to hold whatever you want to turn. The axle must move with the imaginary wheel that the wrench handle makes as you turn it.

You can see that a wheel and axle does not change the direction of your force. As you turn the wheel, the axle turns in the same direction.

An outdoor water faucet often has a handle that fits snugly over the top of a square-ended rod just as a wrench fits a nut. The handle is removed when the faucet isn't being used. It's very hard to turn

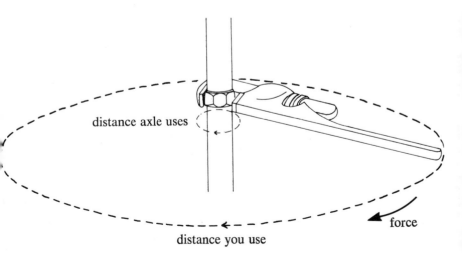

distance axle uses

force

distance you use

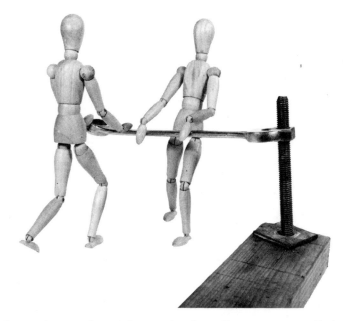

the rod or axle without the handle, as you will discover if you ever lose the handle! If the handle gets lost, you'll probably have to use a pair of pliers as a wheel and axle. The handles of the pliers are turned in a circle, making an imaginary wheel, with the gripping ends holding the axle firmly so that it turns as the wheel turns. Remember, a pair of pliers is two levers. So when you turn on a faucet with a pair of pliers, you are using two kinds of simple machine.

You can use a wheel and axle in the opposite way, trading force for distance. By turning the

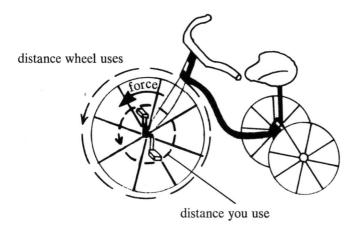

distance wheel uses

force

distance you use

axle you get more distance or speed as the wheel turns. When you ride a tricycle you pump the pedals in a small circle and the large front wheel turns through more distance. This increases your speed since both "wheels" turn in the same amount of time.

You can also feel this increased speed when you play crack-the-whip. In this game the player standing in the center of the "wheel" is the "axle." This player uses force to pull the others around, but he doesn't move through much distance, while the player on the outside end moves very fast through a lot of distance. A cowboy's lasso works the same way. Force is traded for distance as his hand turns the rope in a small circle (the axle) and the loop goes around in a much larger circle or wheel.

**39**

# 6
# Pulleys

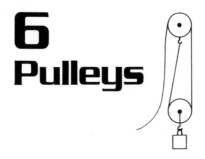

A pulley is a small wheel with a grooved rim that holds a cord or rope. Pulleys can be used in two different ways, either as fixed pulleys or as movable pulleys.

In a fixed pulley, the small wheel turns, but the whole pulley is attached to a wall or other surface so it can't move. In a movable pulley, the whole pulley moves up and down as you pull on the rope. Movable pulleys are simple machines that help you do work by trading distance for force.

Fixed pulleys by themselves do not help you do work; they do not increase or decrease the force or the distance you must use. They are useful, however, because they can change the direction of your force.

A sailboat's mast has a fixed pulley at the top. The rope goes through the pulley. As you pull down on your end of the rope, the other end of the rope goes up, drawing the sail up with it. Flagpoles also have fixed pulleys that change the direction of your force. It is much more convenient to stand on the ground and pull down than to sit on the top of the flagpole and pull up.

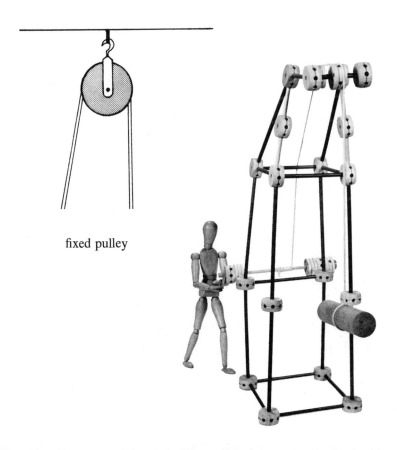

fixed pulley

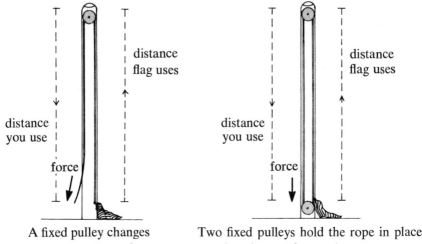

A fixed pulley changes
the direction of your force.

Two fixed pulleys hold the rope in place
but do not change the amount
of distance you must use.

You could pass the rope through a ring or hole at the top of the flagpole and it would work just like a fixed pulley. But because of friction, the rope would soon begin to fray. The pulley wheel turns as the rope is pulled, and friction is reduced.

If you add another fixed pulley near the bottom of the flagpole, the rope can make a loop around both pulleys. Window drapes are often opened and closed by two fixed pulleys in this way. But even two fixed pulleys can change only the direction of your force. In order to change the amount of force or distance you must use, you need a movable pulley.

Machines that are called movable pulleys are often sets of two or more pulley wheels, including both fixed and movable pulleys. But even a single movable pulley is a simple machine that allows you to use less force while you pull the rope through more distance. Even if you don't have any pulley wheels, you can see for yourself how this works. You need a shopping bag filled with books or other heavy things and a piece of rope about twenty feet or six meters long. Before you start, pick up the bag to get an idea of how hard it is to lift.

First try lifting the bag with a fixed pulley. Tie one end of the rope to the bag's handles and bring the other end over the clothes bar of a closet. Use chalk or a piece of string to mark the point on the rope where you start pulling. Now pull down on your end of the rope until the bag is lifted up to the clothes bar. Mark the point on the rope where you stop pulling. Measure how far you have pulled the rope. It will be the same distance that the bag moves. The fixed pulley does not change the distance used. You will probably also notice that you

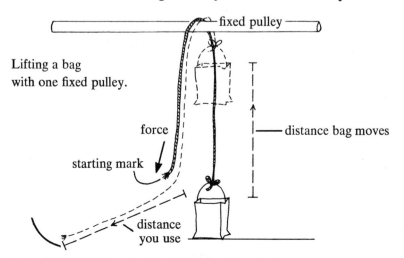

Lifting a bag with one fixed pulley.

fixed pulley

force

starting mark

distance you use

distance bag moves

need about as much force to raise the bag with the fixed pulley as to lift it up to the clothes bar without the pulley. It may seem a little easier to use the pulley because it's easier to pull things down than up. But the fixed pulley does not change the force or the distance needed.

Now try lifting the bag with one movable pulley. Tie one end of the rope to the clothes bar of the closet. Then bring the other end through the bag's handles and back up to the clothes bar. The bag's handles will act as a movable pulley. Now pull up on your end of the rope until the bag is lifted as far as the bar. You'll probably have to stand on a chair to do this. You can see that a single movable pulley does not change the direction of your force. Measure how much rope you have to pull to raise the bag up to the bar. It will be twice the distance that the bag moves, but the bag will feel only half as heavy.

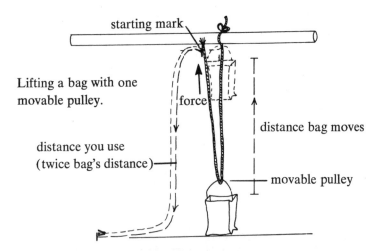

starting mark

Lifting a bag with one movable pulley.

force

distance bag moves

distance you use (twice bag's distance)

movable pulley

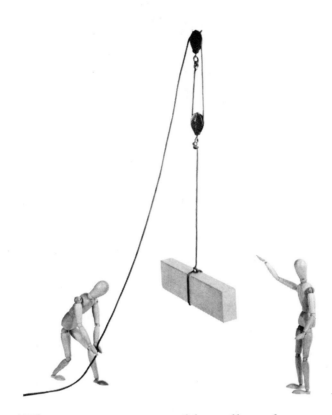

When you use a movable pulley, the two sec-
tions of rope each hold up half the weight you are
lifting. The weight is divided between your hand
on one side and the clothes bar on the other. This
is like two people sharing the weight of a heavy
suitcase. So a movable pulley needs less force, but
you must pull the rope through more distance.

Instead of standing on a chair, you can loop
your end of the rope over the clothes bar and down
to the floor again. Then you have a combination of

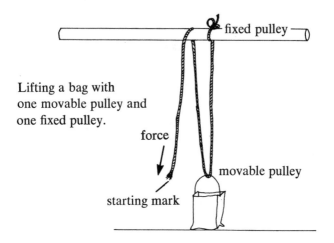

Lifting a bag with
one movable pulley and
one fixed pulley.

fixed pulley

force

movable pulley

starting mark

a fixed and a movable pulley. The fixed pulley lets you pull down instead of up, but it doesn't change the force or the distance you use with the movable pulley.

If you use real pulleys in this experiment, it will feel even easier to lift the bag; real pulleys reduce the friction of the rope on the bar and the bag's handles.

If you have enough rope you can try looping it

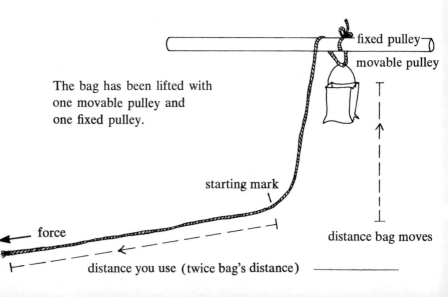

fixed pulley

movable pulley

The bag has been lifted with
one movable pulley and
one fixed pulley.

starting mark

force

distance bag moves

distance you use (twice bag's distance)

through the handles and over the bar again. This is like using two movable pulleys and two fixed pulleys. This time you will have to pull the rope four times as far as the bag moves, but you will only need to use one fourth as much force.

Now you can see how a window washer or a painter can easily pull himself and his equipment

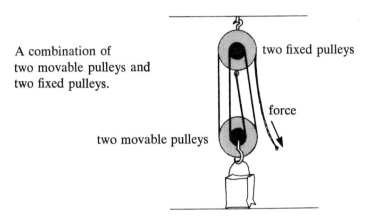

A combination of two movable pulleys and two fixed pulleys.

two fixed pulleys

force

two movable pulleys

up the side of a building. He uses sets of movable pulleys attached to his scaffold and sets of fixed pulleys attached to the building. He uses real pulley wheels not only to keep the ropes from fraying but because the grooved rims hold the ropes in place and keep them from slipping off the pulleys.

Combinations of pulleys are used for many lifting jobs. Pianos and heavy furniture can be moved through an upper story window and boats can be loaded and unloaded with sets of pulleys.

47

# 7
# Screws

A screw is an inclined plane wrapped around a cylinder. The inclined plane forms ridges in a spiral along the cylinder. These ridges are called the threads of the screw.

Using a pencil and a piece of paper, you can show that the threads really are an inclined plane. Make a paper triangle by folding the top edge of a piece of notebook paper over to line up exactly with the right-hand edge. Cut or tear along the fold to make the triangle. The cut edge is an inclined plane. Lay the pencil along the bottom edge and roll up the paper around it. You can see

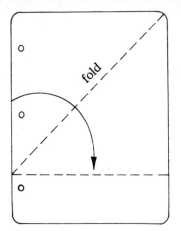

Fold the top edge of the paper to line up with the right-hand edge.

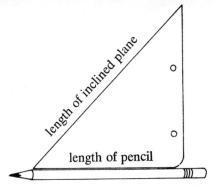

Lay the pencil along the bottom edge of the triangle of paper.

The inclined plane of the paper makes a screw as you roll it around the pencil.

how the inclined plane forms a spiral along the cylinder, although the edge of the paper is much flatter than the threads of a real screw.

You can see that the inclined plane (the cut edge of the paper) is longer than the pencil. If the pencil were a nail, it would use less distance in going into a piece of wood than a screw of the same length. The threads or inclined plane of the screw move through more distance than the edge of the nail, but a screw needs less force. You are trading distance for force.

In order to do work, a screw must be turned. When you turn a screw with a screwdriver, you are using a wheel and axle. The handle is the wheel and the shaft plus the screw are the axle. It's easier

49

to turn the large handle than to turn the shaft or the screw by itself, but you must turn it through more distance.

To see for yourself how a screw helps you do work, you need:

> a block of soft wood
> a wood screw
> a screwdriver
> a nail
> a claw hammer

Be sure the nail is about the same length and thickness as the screw.

First pound the nail into the wood. To start the nail, tap it lightly a few times with the hammer so that the wedge or pointed end of the nail makes a small hole. Then pound the nail all the way in.

Now put the screw into the wood. Again tap it lightly a few times to start the hole. The point of a wood screw is a wedge that makes this easier. Then turn the screw all the way in. You will find that you need less force with the screw than with the nail, but it may take more time because you must use more distance.

50

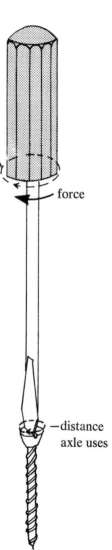

distance you use

force

—distance axle uses

The screwdriver is a wheel and axle to turn the screw.

The turning motion of a screw pulls the wood up the inclined plane of the threads. You do not have to push the screw in—you only have to turn the inclined plane by using the wheel and axle. The edge of this inclined plane is a wedge. As a wood screw turns, the wedge cuts into the wood and makes grooves that exactly fit the threads. So a wood screw combines an inclined plane, a wheel and axle, and a wedge in one simple machine. But the way this machine works is different from the way any other simple machine works.

Besides letting you use less force, a screw changes the direction of your force. Your force goes around the wheel, and the screw goes straight into the wood.

Wood screws are very useful because they hold things together better than nails do. The grooves that the threads cut into the wood hold the screw firmly without slipping. If you try to take out the nail and the screw, you will find this out for yourself.

You must use more distance to put the screw into the wood.

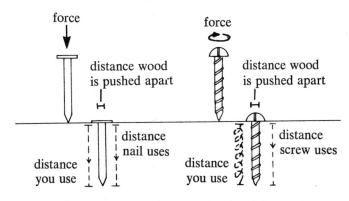

If the head of the nail is flat against the wood, you will have to use a wedge, such as the end of the screwdriver or the tip of the hammer's claw, to raise it a little bit. Then you can use the claw hammer to lever the nail out. It slides out easily. But if you try to do this with the screw, you probably won't have enough force to lever it straight out. The nail needed some force to go in a short distance, but the screw needed less force and more distance to go in as far as the nail. To lever the screw straight out would need much more force for a shorter distance. When you unscrew the screw, again you use less force but more distance. To see how much more distance you used, wrap a piece of string around the screw, following the threads, and then compare this length with the straight length of the nail.

A hand drill is a screw that is used to make holes in wood. As you turn the handle around an imaginary wheel, the drill turns and goes into the

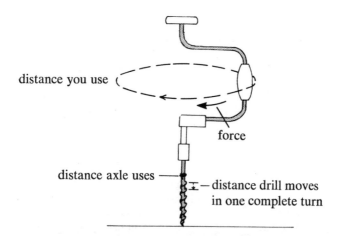

distance you use

force

distance axle uses

distance drill moves in one complete turn

wood along its inclined plane. This is like using a screwdriver to turn a screw. But the handle of the drill uses more distance than a screwdriver's handle, and this means you need less force to turn it.

Screws can also be used as simple machines to lift things. A jackscrew can help lift very heavy things, such as houses, that you could never lift by yourself.

In a jackscrew, the screw fits into a base that has grooves for the screw threads. The base rests on the ground and the screw is turned as far into the base as it can go. The house rests on a platform on top of the screw. A handle is used as a wheel to turn the axle or screw cylinder. As the handle is turned, the screw moves up along the grooved inclined plane of the base and pushes the platform up.

You can make a small jackscrew to find out how it works. You need a long bolt with threads almost up to the head, a small square of card-

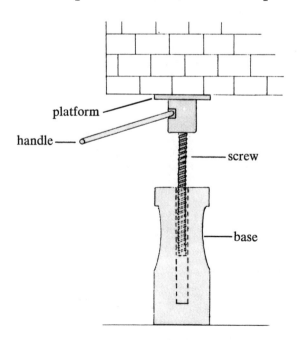

board, and four nuts that fit the bolt. First make a hole a little bigger than the bolt in the middle of the cardboard. Put the bolt through the hole—the cardboard will be the jackscrew's platform. Then screw one of the nuts all the way to the top of the threads as tightly as you can. Attach the other three nuts together with rubber bands or strong glue so they work together like one very thick nut. This will be the base of your jackscrew. Put it on a flat surface and screw the bolt into the base as far as it will go.

Now attach a pipecleaner or piece of wire to the nut at the top of the screw. This makes the handle for turning the jackscrew. Put a piece of modeling clay or a small toy on the platform—this will be the weight you will lift.

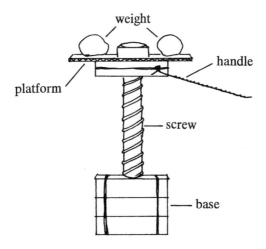

Now hold the base firmly and turn the handle. As you turn the handle through a circle that is an imaginary wheel, the axle, or screw cylinder, turns. The screw moves up the inclined plane of the grooves inside the base and raises the weight.

Remember that the two parts of work are force and distance. To lift the weight straight up would need more force but it would move through less distance. The jackscrew, like any inclined plane, lets you do work with less force but you must use the force through more distance.

In any inclined plane the shallower the angle of slope, the less force is needed, but the distance is increased. In a screw the angle of slope of the

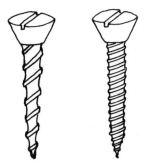

The screw on the right has a shallower pitch than the one on the left.

inclined plane or threads is called pitch. A screw with shallower or smaller pitch moves through a lot of distance but it needs little force.

A piano stool is like a jackscrew, except that the platform to hold the weight is not separate from the wheel. So the weight and the platform turn as the screw turns.

You can lift your mother or father by using a piano stool. When your mother sits on the stool you can turn the outer rim of the wheel and the screw will lift her. You have to turn through more distance than you would need to lift her straight up, but you need much less force.

Like the bolt and the jackscrew, the screw of the piano stool does not have a pointed end. These screws do not need wedges to make holes. Also, their threads do not have to cut grooves as they

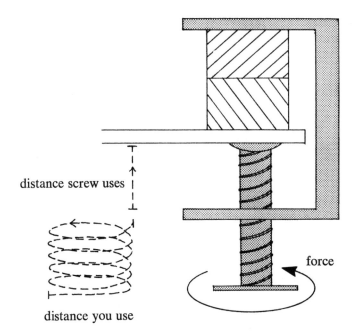

distance screw uses

distance you use

force

move; they move along grooves that are already made in the nuts. So the threads do not need to be wedges either.

A vise or clamp works like a jackscrew, too, but it is used for holding things together instead of for lifting heavy weights. As you turn the handle of the screw around and around, the screw pushes the platform against the objects you want to hold. By using more distance to turn the screw, you can apply more force to hold things together than you could by pushing them together with your hands.

The jaws of a monkey wrench work like a small vise as you use the screw to tighten them.

The screw is a simple machine that can be used in many ways. A jar with a screw-on lid is a simple machine in which the jar is the screw and the lid is the nut. As you know, it is hard to push an ordinary lid on tight enough so that it won't come off. With a screw-on lid, you need much less force to put it on tight, but you must turn it through more distance. And of course the same is true when you take the lid off. You usually

need a lever like a bottle opener to remove an ordinary lid. Removing a screw-on lid requires more distance but you can use your own force; you don't need a lever to help you do this work.

A meat grinder is another kind of screw. When you turn the handle or wheel of a meat grinder, the meat is pushed up the inclined plane of the screw and forced through the holes at the end. It would be difficult, if not impossible, to push the meat through the holes with your hand. You are trading the distance you turn the handle for more force.

Every time you use a tool to do work, you are using a simple machine, or maybe more than one. Kitchen tools, repairing tools, gardening tools, and many toys and games can all help you use your own power more efficiently by trading force for distance or distance for force.

Even machines that are run by motors are often made up of one or more simple machines. Of course a motor provides much more force to run a machine than a person does. But the moving parts of a motor-powered machine may be wheels and axles, screws, or other simple machines.

Next time you use a machine or a tool, see if you

can figure out what kind of simple machine it is. You may be surprised at how many you use every day. And maybe you can think of a way to improve the machine to make the work you're doing even easier. That's the whole idea of simple machines.

# Index